The Thomas Starr King Dispute

For Leo Ribuffo,
Professor of History and Raconteur

The Thomas Starr King Dispute

Acceptance and Unveiling of the Statues of Junipero Serra and Thomas Starr King

Edited and Introduced by Paul J Rich

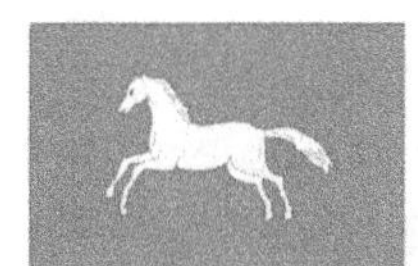

WESTPHALIA PRESS
An imprint of Policy Studies Organization

The Thomas Starr King Dispute
Acceptance and Unveiling of the Statues of Junipero Serra and Thomas Starr King

Westphalia Press
An imprint of Policy Studies Organization
dgutierrezs@ipsonet.org

For information:
Westphalia Press
1527 New Hampshire Ave., N.W.
Washington, D.C. 20036

ISBN-13: 978-0-944285-78-7
ISBN-10: 0944285783

Updated material and comments on this edition can be found at the Policy Studies Organization website:
http://www.ipsonet.org

THE THOMAS STARR KING DISPUTE: PREFACE TO THIS EDITION

A feature of the Capitol in Washington is the collection of statues representing each state. Normally a state may have two of its worthies on display, and in case of California for many years they had been Junipero Serra and Thomas Starr King. Visitors from California could be seen getting their pictures taken in front of one or the other.

In 2006, the California Legislature decided to remove the statue of Thomas Starr King and replace it with a statue of Ronald Reagan. Of course Ronald Reagan is not unnoticed in Washington and represented by a statue at the airport named after him, by several paintings in the Congressional offices, and by the giving of his name to a massive Federal office complex.

In removing Starr King, one reason offered was that he was not born in California. Ronald Reagan was born in Illinois and Father Serra was born in Majorca, so that seemed a spurious excuse. About the affair, the Los Angeles Times (May 29, 2009), commented:

"It's never pleasant watching politicians try to manipulate history. Whether it's an ex-president blocking release of incriminating White House tapes, the Russian government closing a KGB archive to foreign researchers or Japanese officials forcing a school textbook author to excise references to World War II-era atrocities, the public's ability to learn the truth about historic events is hobbled.

The imminent removal from the U.S. Capitol of a statue of Thomas Starr King, a charismatic San Francisco minister and orator credited with helping keep California in the Union during the run-up to the Civil War, hardly qualifies as a major crime against history. Yet the successful effort by California Republicans to replace him in the National Statuary Hall Collection with a larger-than-life sculpture of Ronald Reagan is troubling nonetheless."

It remains troubling that history can become a political football. When the statue was dedicated, its placement was done with great honor and dignity. A new edition of the proceedings of then may give some pause about the furtive way it was removed.

Paul J. Rich

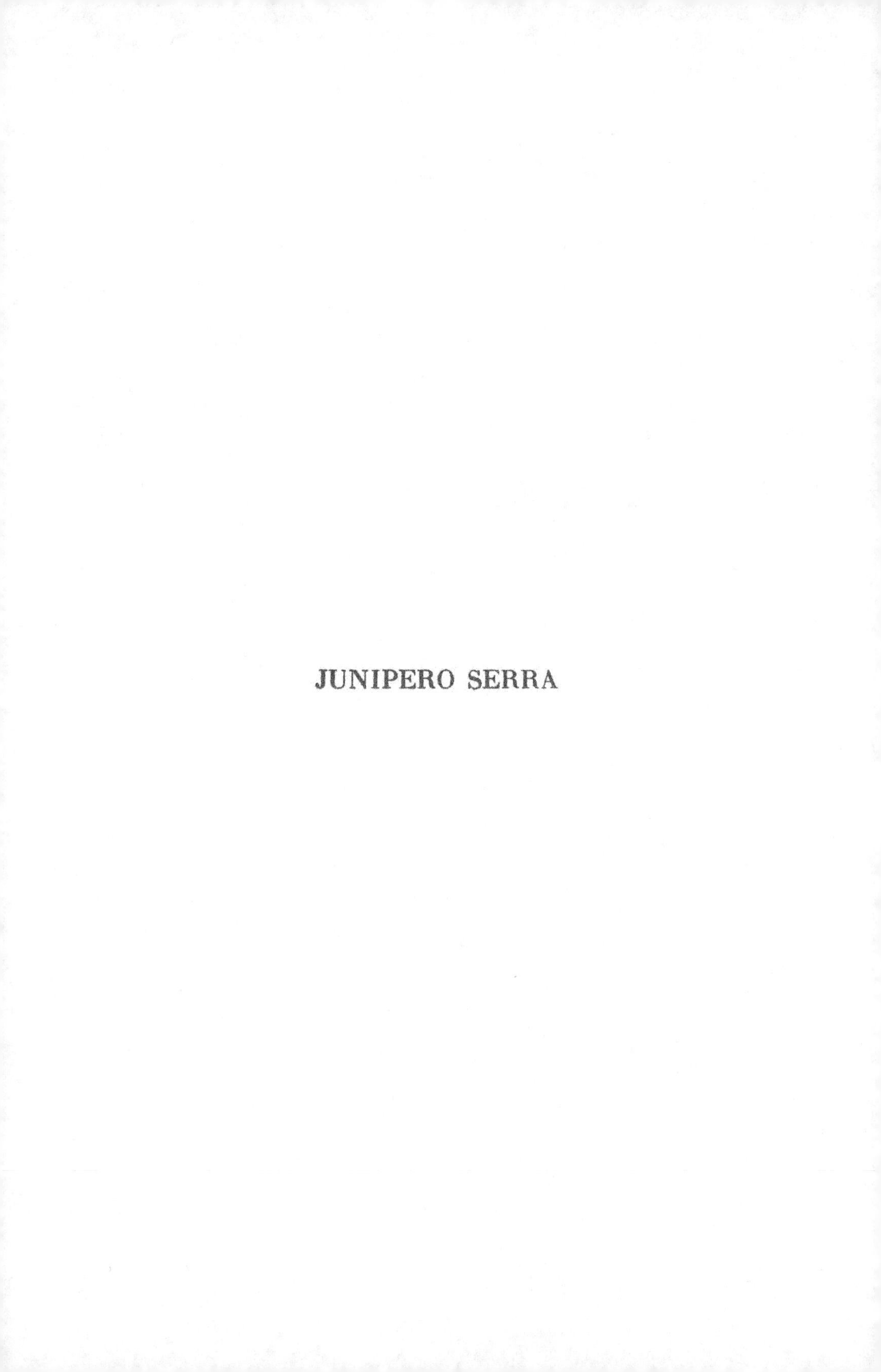

JUNIPERO SERRA

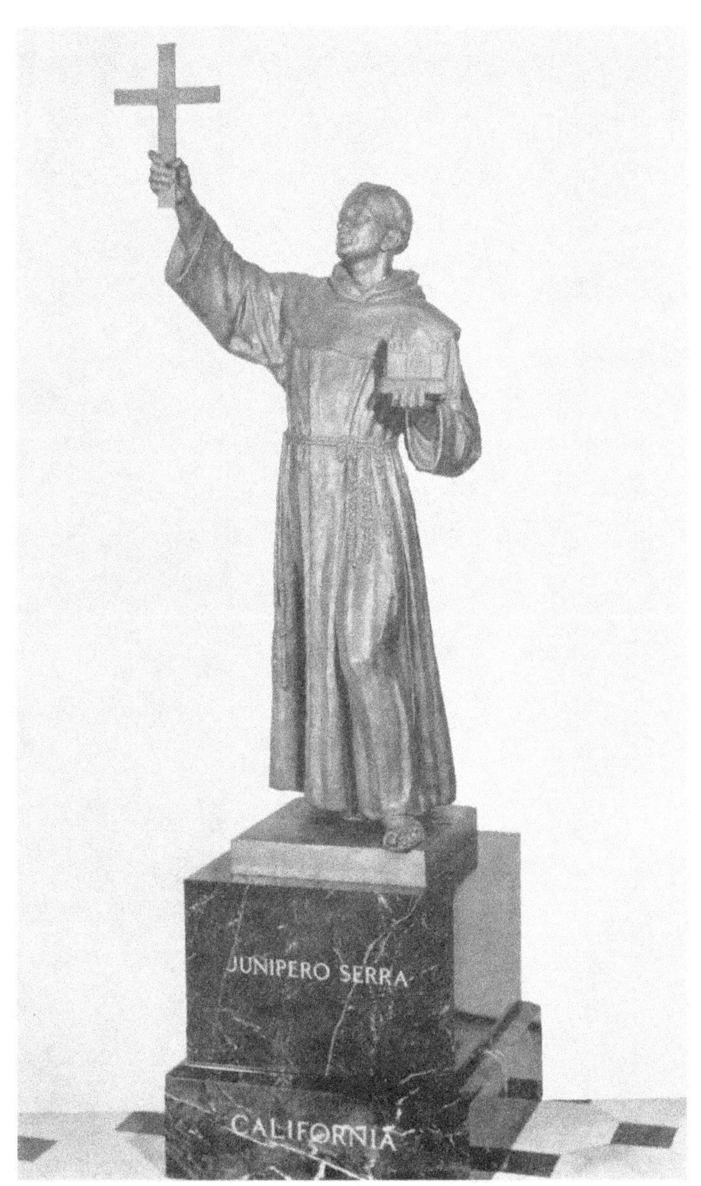
JUNIPERO SERRA
CALIFORNIA

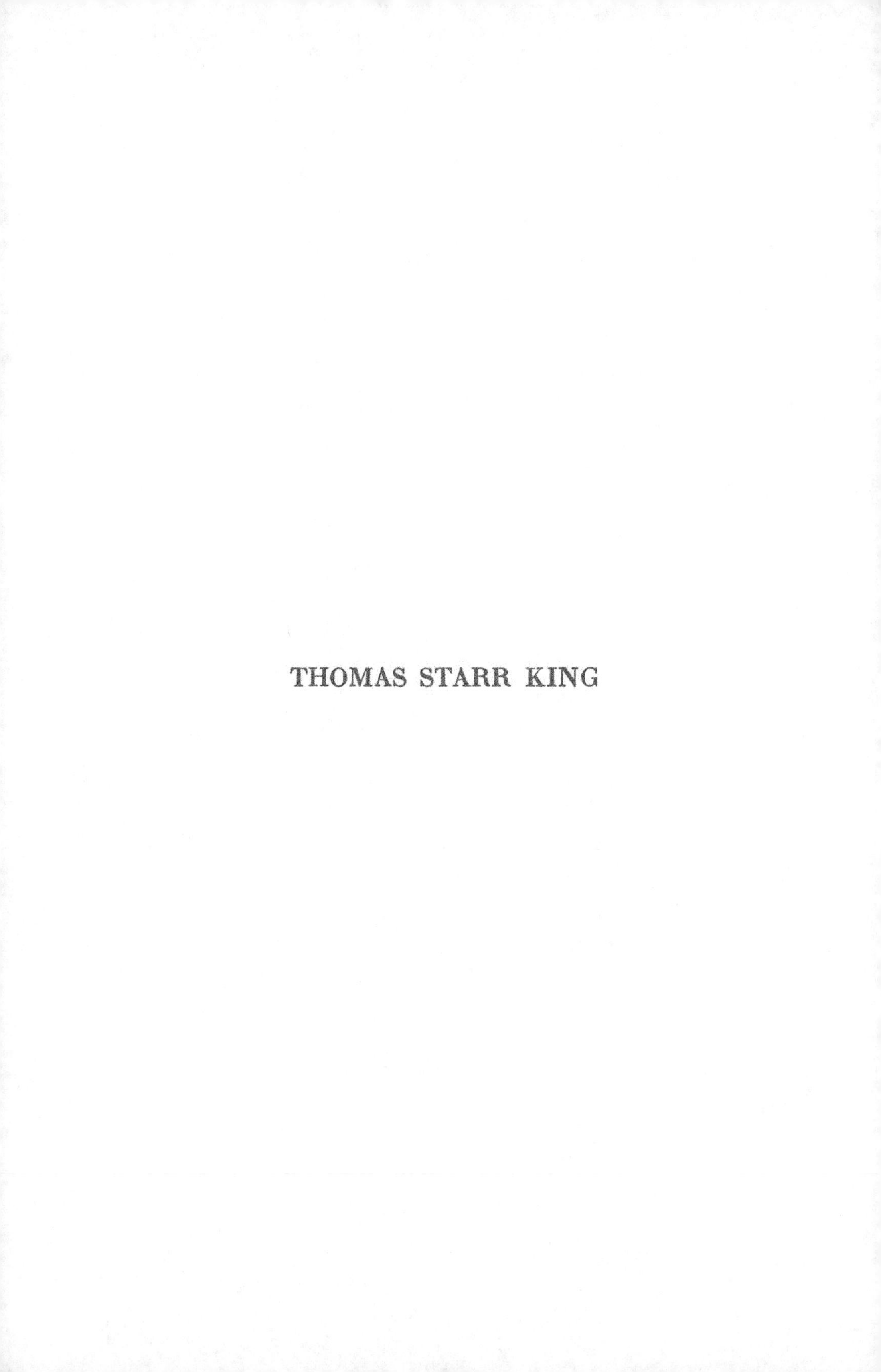

THOMAS STARR KING

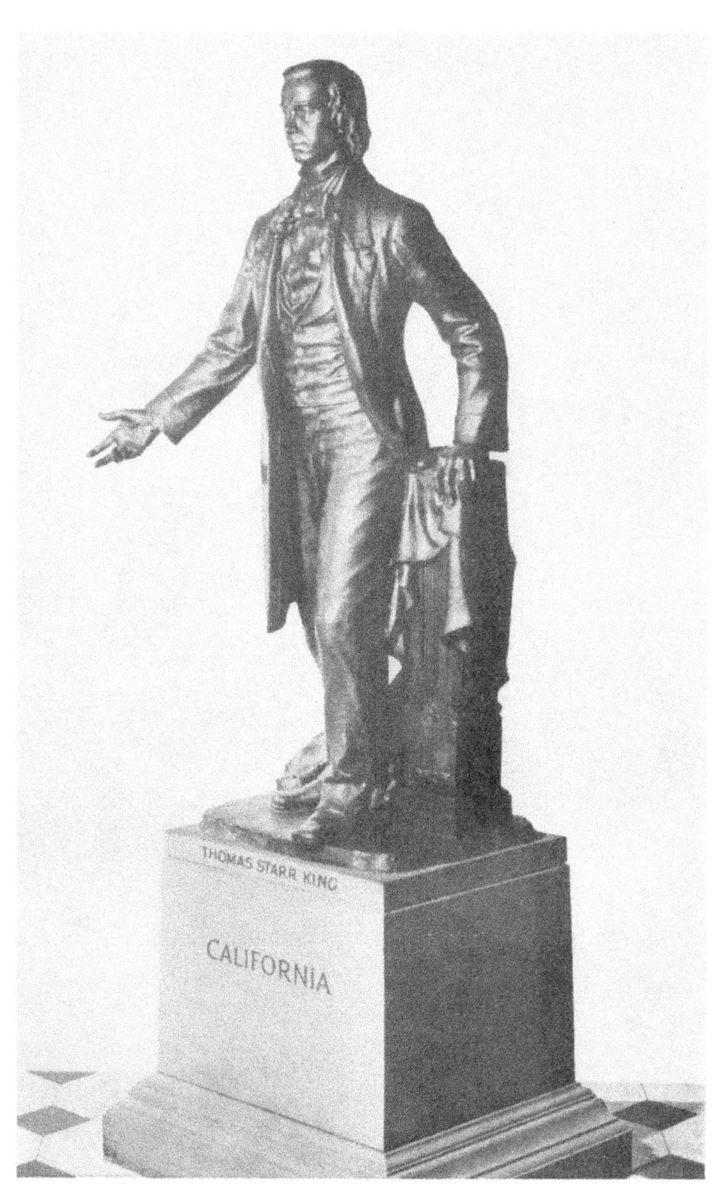
THOMAS STARR KING
CALIFORNIA

72d Congress, 1st Session—Senate Document No. 102

Acceptance and Unveiling of the Statues of

Junipero Serra

and

Thomas Starr King

❧

Presented by the
State of California

❧

Proceedings in the Congress
and in Statuary Hall
United States Capitol

PREPARED UNDER THE DIRECTION OF
THE JOINT COMMITTEE ON PRINTING

CONTENTS

SENATE CONCURRENT RESOLUTION No. 21

SUBMITTED BY MR. SHORTRIDGE

Resolved by the Senate (the House of Representatives concurring), That there be printed with illustrations and bound five thousand copies of the proceedings in Congress, together with the proceedings held at the unveiling in Statuary Hall, upon the acceptance of the statues of JUNIPERO SERRA and THOMAS STARR KING, presented by the State of California, of which one thousand shall be for the use of the Senate and two thousand five hundred for the use of the House of Representatives, and the remaining one thousand five hundred copies shall be for the use and distribution of the Senators and Representatives in Congress from the State of California.

The Joint Committee on Printing is hereby authorized to have the copy prepared for the Public Printer and shall procure suitable illustrations to be published with these proceedings.

Adopted June 11, 1932.

BIOGRAPHY

Junipero Serra was born at Petra, on the island of Majorca, on November 24, 1713; entered the Franciscan Order in 1729 and became a professor in the Lullian University at Palma; crossed the Atlantic Ocean to Vera Cruz, Mexico, in 1749, and entered the College of San Fernando, at Mexico City; was sent as a missionary to the Indians of the Serra Gorda in 1750; went to Lower California in 1769 and established a number of missions both there and in Upper California; founded the first mission in the present State at San Diego; made his headquarters at San Carlos de Carmel, near Monterey, Calif., where he died in 1784; interment beneath the arches of the mission.

139696—32——2

BIOGRAPHY

THOMAS STARR KING was born in New York City, December 17, 1824; moved with his parents to Charlestown, Mass., in 1835; worked as a grocery clerk from 1836 to 1840, when he became an assistant teacher in the Bunker Hill Grammar School, and was made principal of the West Grammar School, at Medford, Mass., in 1842; through self-directed study prepared himself for the ministry and was ordained in 1846; moved to Boston in 1848 and to San Francisco in 1860, continuing his religious work both from the pulpit and the lecture platform; during the Civil War organized the Pacific Coast Sanitary Commission; died in San Francisco, Calif., March 4, 1864.

CALIFORNIA COMMISSION ON REPRESENTATION IN NATIONAL STATUARY HALL

The late Hon. JOHN F. DAVIS
Past Grand President, Native Sons of the Golden West

HEBBERT E. BOLTON, Ph.D., LL. D.
University of California

The late Mrs. FRANK A. GIBSON
California Federation of Women's Clubs

Miss MABEL R. GILLIS
State Librarian

Miss GRACE S. STOERMER
Past Grand President, Native Daughters of the Golden West

STATE OFFICIALS

JAMES ROLPH, Jr., *Governor*
FRANK F. MERRIAM, *Lieutenant Governor*
FRANK C. JORDAN, *Secretary of State*
U. S. WEBB, *Attorney General*
RAY L. RILEY, *Controller*
CHARLES G. JOHNSON, *Treasurer*

THE SCULPTORS

Ettore Cadorin was born in Venice, Italy, March 1, 1876. He received his art education in the Royal Academy of Fine Arts, in Venice, where he was awarded two first medals and scholarships; at the School of Applied Arts, and in the studio of his father. He came to the United States in 1912; was professor of literature and art at Columbia University from 1915 to 1917; the official representative of the Italian Government in this country as lecturer in art in 1918 and 1919, and teacher of sculpture in Santa Barbara (Calif.) State Teachers College from 1926 to 1929. Mr. Cadorin is a member of the National Sculpture Society and the Beaux Arts Institute of Design. Among his principal works are two colossal statues in St. Marks Square, Venice; the Wagner Memorial, Venice; ivory portraits of royal princesses of Italy; war memorial, Edgewater, N. J.; statuary for courthouse at Santa Barbara, Calif.; and the statue of Junipero Serra in Statuary Hall.

Haig Patigian was born in Van, Armenia, January 22, 1876. His early education was under his parents who were teachers in the schools of American Missions; self educated in art, he devoted himself to sculpture after working three years as a newspaper artist. In 1906 and 1907 he worked in Paris, with Alix Marquet as an occasional critic. In 1907 his allegorical statue, Ancient History, was exhibited in the Salon des Artistes Français. Honors, Hors Concours, Member of Jury, Panama Pacific International Exposition, 1915; awarded medal for distinguished services in the Department of Fine Arts. Member National Institute of Arts and Letters, National Sculpture Society Société des Artistes Français. Among his principal works are McKinley monument, Arcata, Calif.; Dolbeer memorial, San Francisco; Rowell monument, Fresno, Calif.; allegorical figures of Imagination, Invention, Steam Power, Electricity, and other works of sculpture for the Panama Pacific International Exposition; including Vanity (marble); Apollo and Diana; busts of Lieut. Gov. John M. Eshleman, University of California; General Funston, City Hall, San Francisco; Pediment of Metropolitan Life Building, San Francisco; Tympanium group of arts, sciences, etc., for the Memorial Museum, San Francisco; heroic statue of Lincoln, in the Civic Center, and of General Pershing, in the Golden Gate Park, San Francisco; bust of Herbert Hoover, White House, Washington, D. C.; the Alden J. Blethen Memorial, Seattle, Wash.; and the statue of Thomas Starr King in Statuary Hall.

CONGRESSIONAL DELEGATION FROM CALIFORNIA

SENATORS

Hon. Hiram W. Johnson
Hon. Samuel M. Shortridge

REPRESENTATIVES

Hon. Clarence F. Lea
Hon. Harry L. Englebright
Hon. Charles F. Curry, Jr.
Hon. Florence P. Kahn
Hon. Richard J. Welch
Hon. Albert E. Carter
Hon. Henry E. Barbour
Hon. Arthur M. Free
Hon. William E. Evans
Hon. Joe Crail
Hon. Philip D. Swing

UNVEILING *and* PRESENTATION

Statuary Hall, March 1, 1931

PROGRAM OF EXERCISES

Music—2.30–3.00 . . . UNITED STATES MARINE BAND
Capt. TAYLOR BRANSON, *Leader*

Miss GRACE S. STOERMER
Secretary California Commission, *Presiding*

Favorite Selections of Junipero Serra and Thomas Starr King . . . . UNITED STATES MARINE BAND

Invocation . . . Rt. Rev. Bishop THOMAS J. SHAHAN
Rector Emeritus of the Catholic University of America

Introductory Remarks . . . . . PRESIDING OFFICER

Presentation of Statues . . . Hon. HIRAM W. JOHNSON

Unveiling of Statue—Junipero Serra—
Hon. FLORENCE PRAG KAHN

Unveiling of Statue—Thomas Starr King—
THOMAS STARR KING
Lieut. Commander United States Navy
(Grandson of Thomas Starr King)

Acceptance on behalf of the Government—
THE PRESIDENT'S REPRESENTATIVE

" Star-Spangled Banner " . UNITED STATES MARINE BAND

Address—Junipero Serra . Hon. ISIDORE B. DOCKWEILER

Selection . . . . . . UNITED STATES MARINE BAND

Address—Thomas Starr King—
Hon. SAMUEL M. SHORTRIDGE

"America " . . . . . . UNITED STATES MARINE BAND

Brief Tributes . . . . Mrs. WILLIAM ELMER EVANS; Hon. ARTHUR M. FREE; Father SERAPHIN MULLER

" I Love You, California " . UNITED STATES MARINE BAND

Benediction . . . . Rev. ULYSSES GRANT PIERCE
Pastor of the Unitarian Church, Washington, D. C.

" Stars and Stripes Forever "—
UNITED STATES MARINE BAND

Statue of Junipero Serra sculptured by
ETTORE CADORIN
Santa Barbara, California

Statue of Thomas Starr King sculptured by
HAIG PATIGIAN
San Francisco, California

Grateful acknowledgment is made of helpful assistance rendered by the office of the Architect of the Capitol for the preparation and arrangements for the ceremonies in Statuary Hall.

STATUES OF SERRA AND KING

SUNDAY, *March 1, 1931.*

The presentation and unveiling of the statues of JUNIPERO SERRA and THOMAS STARR KING, of California, was held in Statuary Hall, United States Capitol, Washington, D. C., on Sunday, March 1, 1931, at three o'clock p. m.

Miss Grace S. Stoermer, secretary of the California Commission on Representation in National Statuary Hall, presided.

Several selections were rendered by the United States Marine Band, Capt. Taylor Branson, leader.

The PRESIDING OFFICER. In the absence of His Grace, Most Reverend Michael J. Curley, Archbishop of the Diocese of Baltimore, I am privileged to present to you, Right Reverend Bishop Thomas J. Shahan, D. D., Rector Emeritus of the Catholic University of America and one of our country's finest historians, who will give the invocation. Bishop Shahan.

INVOCATION

Bless, we beseech Thee, O God of our fathers, these precious memorials, wrought with rare skill and in sincere faith, by which Thy children of California would commend to their fellow citizens of this great Republic the merits and services of two men to whom this sovereign State is so deeply indebted that only in the immortal coin of gratitude can it hope to satisfy in some measure its many and great obligations.

Thou alone knowest, Eternal Father, amid what hardships Thy servant Junipero Serra spread among savage men, little better than animals, the saving truths of the Gospel of Thy Son Jesus Christ; what zeal and fortitude, what confidence in Thee, what patience and self-denial sustained him in journeys innumerable, through trackless forests and across endless wastes, sustained ever by invincible faith in Thee, inspired by his love for perishing souls, and rewarded by Thy comforting and enlightening presence.

Thou knowest, O Lord, what seeds of civilization both he and his courageous companions sowed in the hearts and minds of ignorant and debased men, and how in due time its fruits, sown amid tears and trials, were reaped in joy. The hard trails that his weary feet traversed are to-day a royal road along which are strung great cities, on which nature exhibits all her riches, and human progress its every latest attainment.

We believe, indeed, O Lord, that Thy servant rejoices in Thy bosom at so much magnificence of life, but we believe also that he rejoices even more in the energy and grandeur of the spiritual life that now prospers so richly where he found only moral desolation and the last vestiges of human welfare.

To Thee also, O Lord, are known the splendid civic merits of Thomas Starr King, foremost of the sons of California in the service of our glorious American Union during dark days of war and its many afflictions and sufferings. To his faith in the Union, his incomparable eloquence, his ingenious activity, and his farseeing charity California offers her tribute of gratitude as to one who chose the highest way of our everyday life, devotion of self to the common welfare, counting life itself as a sacrifice that the common weal may rightly demand in a crucial hour, but at the price of eternal reverence for the generous donor.

The PRESIDING OFFICER. It is a joy and a privilege to stand in Statuary Hall in the historic city of Washington, the Capital of our own United States, and gaze on the magnificent statuary commemorative of the illustrious and great citizens of our country.

It is gratifying in this commercial and industrial age to know that there are those who are interested in the artistic and cultural features of civilization. Reviewing our history we find that in 1864, at the suggestion of Senator Morrill of Vermont, the old House of Representatives was set apart as National Statuary Hall to which each State was invited to send the statues of two of its most distinguished citizens. The President was authorized to invite the State to provide and furnish statues in marble or bronze, not to exceed two in number, of deceased persons who have been citizens thereof, and illustrious for their historic renown because of distinguished civil or military service, such as each State shall determine to be worthy of this national commemoration.

It has been sixty-seven years since the enactment of this legislation and while California is always in the vanguard in every progressive movement, in

139696—32——3

this particular instance she has been slow in her contribution to this national edifice. Prior to 1927, on several occasions, effort had been made to promote this recognition for California. Each time there had been many differences of opinion as to the logical ones to be selected and a conclusion was never reached. Through the history and landmarks Department of the California Federation of Women's Clubs and the Native Sons and Native Daughters of the Golden West, a state-wide movement was inaugurated after which a bill was passed in the legislature of 1927, providing for the appointment of a commission of five. The names of JUNIPERO SERRA and THOMAS STARR KING were officially approved as California's most distinguished citizens.

We are assembled here to-day to do honor to these men who have brought much recognition and prestige to California.

We are disappointed not to have the Governor of California, James Rolph, jr., with us, but his official duties require his presence at Sacramento as the legislature is in session. He has sent us a word of greeting which it is my privilege to read to you.

STATE OF CALIFORNIA,
GOVERNOR'S OFFICE,
Sacramento, February 25, 1931.

MR. DAVID LYNN,
Architect of the Capitol,
Washington, D. C.

DEAR MR. LYNN: Governor Rolph has requested me to acknowledge and thank you for your kind invitation to be your guest on the occasion of the unveiling of the statues of JUNIPERO SERRA and THOMAS STARR KING in the Statuary Hall of the National Capitol, Washington, D. C., on Sunday afternoon, March 1, at 3 o'clock.

The governor regrets exceedingly his inability to be with you on this occasion due to the many official duties in connection with the legislature which, now in session, requires his presence in Sacramento.

However, the governor wishes for your ceremonies the greatest possible success, and with his compliments and best wishes, I am,

Very sincerely yours,

F. A. COCHRAN,
Executive Secretary.

The PRESIDING OFFICER. I am also happy to read a telegram from the Franciscan Fathers and a letter from Alejandro Padilta, Spanish Ambassador.

[Telegram]

FEBRUARY 27, 1931.

MISS GRACE S. STOERMER,
Secretary of the California Commission
Representation, National Statuary Hall
Washington, D. C.

We are sincerely thankful for the kind invitation and justly proud of the honor which is being bestowed upon Father JUNIPERO SERRA the most representative of all our Franciscan Fathers of the West. Kindly assure the Governor of California and the California Commission that we, the Franciscan Fathers of the Sunshine State, are one with them in their joyful sentiments on Sunday's festive occasion.

FRANCISCAN FATHERS,
REV. GREGORY WOOLER O. F. M.

EMBAJADA DE ESPAÑA,
Washington.

Alejandro Padilla, Spanish Ambassador, presents his compliments to the Governor of California and the California Commission Representation, National Statuary Hall, and begs to thank them for their kind invitation to attend the ceremonies of the unveiling of the statues of JUNIPERO SERRA and THOMAS STARR KING on March 1, 1931, but having received said invitation to-day, February 28, deeply regrets to have taken a previous engagement.

He will be represented by Count de Montefuerte, Minister Counselor to this Royal Spanish Embassy.

WASHINGTON, *February 28, 1931.*

The PRESIDING OFFICER. It is, indeed, an honor to have the privilege of presenting to our audience Hon. Hiram W. Johnson, former governor and now senior Senator from California, who represents the State and the California Commission on Representation. The Honorable Hiram W. Johnson.

ADDRESS BY SENATOR JOHNSON

The State of California availing herself of the privilege extended by a considerate Nation presents to-day, through her governor and her commission appointed for that purpose, the representative of which presides here, statues in bronze of two men, illustrious for their services to their fellow men, and whom the State of California deems worthy of national commemoration.

Neither was either warrior or statesman, but they possessed the highest qualities of both. Each set himself to a task demanding the noblest attribute of human kind, and requiring a courage as lofty as ever displayed upon the field of battle.

Each in self abnegation and sacrifice performed well his task, and both have left their imprint indelible upon a great Commonwealth.

One of these statues commemorates a pure and simple life, devoted to the inculcation of the principles of Christianity and modern civilization in a new land and among a primitive people. JUNIPERO SERRA identified himself with California while California was yet foreign territory, in order to educate, train, and help the Indians dwelling in that region. His work was fundamental and permanent. His teachings and his beneficent example, not only affected for good the people among whom he lived, but have helped and inspired innumerable lives in a great American Commonwealth erected on the scene of his labors.

He was a pioneer of pioneers bringing Christian civilization to a primitive and savage land, now a wondrous empire.

In the other bronze presented to-day, we find expressed the form and features of a man who came to California at the most critical period in her political history.

THOMAS STARR KING at the beginning of the Civil War, found the people of his adopted State, then without transcontinental connection or communication, far removed from the center of discussion, uncertain as to her future course. With dauntless purpose and high enthusiasm, he entered the momentous struggle there, and by his matchless eloquence and indefatigable labors, he contributed in great measure to maintaining California as a member of the Federal Union, and earned for himself the immortal epitaph "He saved his State to the Union."

So now in conformity with the wishes of the people of the State of California, I present, in behalf of California, to the Nation, these two statues, one of JUNIPERO SERRA, and the other of THOMAS STARR KING, to speak by their presence here to all who shall pause to behold them, of successful labors for the lowly, of the virtues of Christian citizenship, and of devotion to the welfare and perpetuity of a Government dedicated to the principles of liberty.

The PRESIDING OFFICER. California is proud and honored in having among its congressional delegation a woman of such marked ability and sterling worth as Hon. Florence Prag Kahn. She has pioneered in the field of governmental activity and responsibility and it is only fitting that she has been selected to unveil the statue of California's first pioneer, JUNIPERO SERRA.

Mrs. Kahn thereupon unveiled the Serra statue.

The PRESIDING OFFICER. This is indeed a happy occasion for to-day we have with us the grandson and namesake of THOMAS STARR KING, as well as four great-grandchildren. When making preparations for the unveiling of the statutes it was our hope that we might find a relative of THOMAS STARR KING, but we were not so optimistic as to think we could locate any near relative. One day a letter came to my desk from a lieutenant commander of the United States Navy at Annapolis, signed THOMAS STARR KING, grandson of the man we are honoring, seeking information as to the dedication ceremonies. Through him we learned that his father, Frederick Randolph King, was living in San Francisco. Both father and son were to have been present to-day, but the father has written us expressing his regret at his inability to be here. It is a joy to have the son with us and it gives me great pleasure to present Thomas Starr King who will unveil the statue of his grandfather.

The statue was unveiled by Lieut. Commander Thomas Starr King.

The PRESIDING OFFICER. We are greatly honored by the presence of Hon. Ray Lyman Wilbur, who is here to represent the President of the United States in the acceptance of these statues. Mr. Secretary Wilbur.

ADDRESS BY SECRETARY WILBUR

The President has asked me to act as his special representative and to deliver the following message:

Junipero Serra, imbued with divine spirit, charged with an exalted mission and sustained by an unfaltering faith, faced with supreme courage, danger, privation, suffering, disease, to carry the message of salvation over unknown paths along the unchartered shores of the Pacific to the hostile, ignorant, lowly Indian dwellers in that wild empire of the West. He was the torch bearer of civilization.

From the silver strand of San Diego to the Golden Gate of San Francisco Bay he planted the holy cross midst the lilies of the field and the wild roses of the valleys, builded missions for the devout, and taught the spiritually helpless and hopeless natives of the forests and plains to turn their faces from the darkness of heathenism toward the celestial light of Christianity and immortality. Heroism, tragedy, despair, and triumph are the milestones that mark "El Camino Real" from mission to mission—that tortuous highway along which this noble and unselfish servant of the Lord unceasingly labored to impart the joy of Christian belief.

Richly endowed with kindness and patience, though thwarted again and again by superstition and savagery, he bravely, zealously, lovingly, and indefatigably remained steadfast in the trust, finally gaining the devotion and respect of those wild children of nature, instructed them in the arts and crafts of the farmer and mechanic and awakened their souls in the name of the Father of all.

The tide of mental enlightenment and spiritual uplift that followed in his wake still rises with the passing of years. His name is reverent, his work enduring, his influence is ever living.

THOMAS STARR KING, preacher-patriot, reared in the cradle of the Revolutionary War, suckled at the breast of freedom, thrilled by the eloquence of Henry Ward Beecher and Wendell Phillips, broadened by the philosophy of Ralph Waldo Emerson—he early in life espoused the cause of freedom for the slaves; then taking the advice of his friend, Horace Greeley, followed the star of empire westward to California a few short years after her admission to the Union of States.

Soon after came the Civil War, each side to that tragic conflict having many friends and sympathizers on the Pacific slope; and then it was that this scholarly, magnetic, witty, radiant orator and devoted follower of Lincoln rode day and night from town to town, from mountain to sea, in that great domain, pleading to preserve the unity of the States, hammering at the shackles of slavery boldly, confidently, brilliantly, captivating the hearts and minds of men, kindling the spirit of "one union indivisible into a living patriotic flame.

He prevailed—but at the expense of life, for all that he had he gave freely, gladly, eagerly, as a Christian statesman, to his cause.

These ambassadors of God, each in his age left his indelible imprint upon the life of that Western land.

Each labored to inculcate the spiritual in the lives of the people of his day. Each was a great leader in a formative period of the State. Each furnished vital contributions to its moral and material foundation. Its admirable structure is builded upon that spiritual, humanitarian, and patriotic foundation, the work of the noble JUNIPERO SERRA and the inspired THOMAS STARR KING.

It is gratifying and appropriate that the images of such men adorn this Hall, and the tender of these beautiful statues by the State of California is accepted by the United States of America.

The United States Marine Band played the " Star Spangled Banner."

The PRESIDING OFFICER. It is a pleasure to introduce Hon. Isidore B. Dockweiler, a native Californian, who will speak on JUNIPERO SERRA. Mr. Dockweiler was born in Los Angeles, through which city runs the El Camino Real—the King's Highway—a road traversed by the sandaled feet of this humble adopted son of California—Father SERRA. The record of the life of this Franciscan is written so indelibly in California's history that his accomplishments and achievements are familiar to all. Hon. Isidore B. Dockweiler.

ADDRESS BY MR. DOCKWEILER

Fellow Citizens: This is a day memorable for the State of California and inspirational for the Nation at large. It is a day of fulfilled duty to the past and of hostages for the future.

Pursuant to the congressional act of 1864 establishing Statuary Hall, a majority of the States have solemnly brought to the Capital and formally presented to the Nation silent replicas in bronze or marble of " deceased persons who have been citizens thereof and illustrious for their historic renown or for distinguished civic or military services " and " such as each State may deem to be worthy of this national commemoration."

They have thus fulfilled a civic duty—old as government—to consecrate the memory of citizens who have served well their native or adopted State. They have thus offered pledges to the future, of ideals to be emulated, and traditions to be cherished, by succeeding generations. They have thus linked the past with the future of our Republic. They have thus justified the faith of the fathers.

The catalogue of statues, thus far given place in this hall of immortals, constitutes an inventory of American achievement in a variety of phases. There are figures which must always stalk conspicuously, though in the silence of death, to and fro upon the stage of our national life. There are figures more retiring and less self-assertive, whose influence must always be more unobtrusive but not less potent. There are figures whose names are household words in the Nation's lexicon. There are figures whose names are of more restricted import and familiarity. But one quality all these immortals have—the quality of singular inspiration.

To-day we have come from the far-flung reaches of California—the spirit of the Conquistadores, the sandal-footed missionaries, the Forty-niners, and the later pioneer generation hovering o'er—to present to the Nation two distinguished Californians, silent in marble but vibrant in their influence exerted upon our beloved State.

I, as spokesman for my native State, am honored to speak what must be at best a faulty and insufficient word of tribute to the first preeminent Californian—a man of greatness in simplicity, of outstanding accomplishment amid discouragement, of untiring zeal in the cause of religion, of unremitting effort on behalf of civilization—the venerable and venerated brown-garbed and sandaled Franciscan friar, JUNIPERO SERRA, worthy follower of his spiritual father, St. Francis of Assisi.

The life story of SERRA is one of inspiring romance. Born at Petra, in the Island of Majorca, Spain, in the year 1713, of parentage poor and pious, he evidenced early in life that instinct of gentleness and piety which complexioned and gave particular charm and luster to his maturer years. At the age of sixteen he entered the service of the Catholic Church, following in the footsteps of the sainted Francis whose attachment to all forms of heaven's simpler creatures is one of the pure romances of the ages. In time he received the title of Doctor of Divinity, and became a professor in the Lullian University, accomplishing "his work," it is related, "with great fame as a man of profound learning." He was distinguished as one of the most eloquent pulpit orators of Europe and was sought after even by the court itself. There is authority for the belief that, had he remained in Spain, he would have become one of the outstanding ecclesiastics of his time, with perhaps cardinal's robes to grace his later years. But SERRA, instinct with apostolic zeal, had his heart set upon missionary work among the benighted natives of the New World.

Forth from Cadiz he ventured—thirty-six years of age—and, landing at Vera Cruz, late in 1749, trudged afoot to the City of Mexico, accompanied by only one companion and without any provisions or guide, relying entirely upon Divine Providence and the hospitality of the inhabitants. During the rough and tedious journey he received a wound in his leg from which he never entirely recovered. Soon he accepted a call to the wild and inhospitable reaches of the Sierra Gorda in Mexico and for nineteen long years ministered to the wandering savages of that vast desolation. His mission became the model mission of the country.

Forth ventured he again in 1769, this new Galahad in quest of the Holy Grail, into the remoter regions of Lower California and then into what at the time was known as Alta California, now simply our beloved California. Portola headed the colonists; SERRA, as father president of the missionaries, headed the band of Franciscans whose historic achievements are the glory and tradition of California. Amid early discouragements and starvation he exclaimed: "Let us speak no more upon the subject; I have placed my faith in God and trust in his goodness to plant the standard of the Holy Cross not only at San Diego but even as far as Monterey." Prophetic words these!

The passing of fifteen years from 1769 saw the establishment by him of nine missions, beginning at San Diego's silver bay in the south and stretching upward to San Francisco's Golden Gate in the north. The impetus thus given did not cease with his death but continued afterwards, and twelve more missions were established, ending farther northward, at Sonoma in the Valley of the Moon. This is the rosary of his service—twenty-one missions for God and government along El Camino Real—The Kings Highway—from San Diego to Sonoma, about seven hundred miles. San Diego de Alcalá, San Carlos de Carmel, San Gabriel, San Antonio de Dadua, San Fernando Rey de España, San Luis Obispo, San Francisco de Assisi, San Juan Capistrano, Santa Clara, San Buenaventura, Santa Barbara, La Purisima Concepcion, La Soledad, Santa Cruz, San Juan Bautista, San Jose de Guadalupe, San Miguel, San Luis Rey de Francia, Santa Ynez, San Rafael, and San Francisco Solano.

What a convocation of memories! Each name redolent of heavenly benediction upon a benighted people! Each name a pillar supporting the glory of an age to come! Each name an epoch in the ebb and flow of time!

For nigh on sixteen years this able, simple, kindly friar toiled in California. Up and down the coast on foot he traveled, an invalid physically. He taught the native Indians the homely arts of husbandry; he instilled into them the rudiments of government in frontier society; he brought to them the civilizing message of Christian belief and ethics. He prepared the slopes of this western land for the advance of empire which years later was to press on and fructify.

He and his fellow friars brought thither, through Old Mexico, over plains and mountains rife with hostile savages, over burning sands of trackless deserts, along a highway marked out by himself, the orange, the lemon, the olive, the fig, the vine, and other fruit-bearing trees, the seed of vegetables and cereals, cattle, sheep, goats, and horses, agricultural implements and the tools of the mechanic.

SERRA found in California a native whose only knowledge of a home or structure was expressed by the primitive "lean-to" of willow branches covered with mud as a protection from inclement weather. But in a few years he caused these same natives to be taught the art of making mortar and cement and brick and tile, the hewing of stone and timber, the fashioning of iron agricultural implements and domestic utensils. These twenty-one mission churches and outlying buildings, some of which still defy time and are the architectural wonder of California, continue to inspire the modern builder to design and build thousands upon thousands of homes, commercial buildings, and public edifices along their graceful and enduring lines. No other section of our country can boast of a series of monuments, built by pioneers—so useful, so characteristic, so picturesque, so intriguing—so challenging.

SERRA was the first to apply within the domain over which the stars and stripes now float the science of irrigation, and the irrigation systems of the missions have always excited the admiration of the hydraulic engineer. It can justly be said that he was the father, in our country, of the science of irrigation. And most certainly he was the great pioneer who revealed to the world the capacities of California's fertile soil and healthful climate, thereby laying the foundation for its subsequent greatness.

Three things of singular importance in the economy of civilization concurred in this period of California's history—the mission, which meant the spread of religion in heathen lands; the presidio, which meant the expansion of the political and military domain of Spain; and the pueblo, or settlement, which meant the establishment of orderly civil government. A tripartite development, in a form worthy of reflection and study even in our own day. A development at once secular and spiritual. The sword supporting the cross; the cross supporting the sword; and both supporting civil authority. What a jointure of effort! What a resultant achievement—despite the disappointment and cupidity that lay in ambush for future years and conspired to severely test, if not blight, the work of the great SERRA.

SERRA represented a theory of colonial government which is obsolete to-day. Yet it exercised profound influence upon the destiny of the world. It was the theory under which Spain acquired one of the great colonial domains of all time, and retained that domain for three centuries and more. What other theory has achieved like results in modern times?

It is for us Americans a matter worthy of most serious reflection that had it not been for the régime of SERRA—that is, the system of mission life which started in 1769 and ended in 1823—this great territory of California might, and likely would, have fallen into the grasp of some other nation and been permanently lost to our Republic. The transition of the California of SERRA to the California of to-day was, as history is interpreted, a normal sequence. SERRA therefore is a legitimate precursor of the later-day civil authorities established by the American Government upon the shores of the Pacific. And such work of preparation accomplished by such a precursor! Lands, peoples; agriculture, horticulture, viticulture; communications, arts, government; hearts, minds, and above all, souls, prepared and tempered and awaiting a later larger development, but a development always predicated upon the previous monumental work of the urbane and saintly padre of the Indians.

While our revolutionary fathers were engaged in their greatest contest for the achievement of political liberty on our eastern shore, Padre SERRA and his brown-robed Franciscans were engaged in the Christianization and civilization of the natives on our western shore.

STATUES OF SERRA AND KING

SERRA is one of the picturesque figures of modern history. No military conqueror, no dominating overlord, no ambitioned statesman, no wizard of any sort, but a sympathetic, zealous, painstaking, able, cultured, highly educated, quiet mannered, undaunted, and unostentatious worker in a pioneer field among primitive peoples, his spirit saturated with love for Jesus Christ and with an eye to the eternal salvation of these peoples and their earthly welfare as well. What a lesson to the vainglorious!

It is said of him that he was not only the guiding spirit in this work of Christianizing and civilizing the Indians but was himself in fact the hardest worker of all. It is likewise said that he chiefly attracted the Indians by his just and paternal treatment and frequently was placed in the necessity of defending their interests when threatened by rapacious civilians. He established a village type of life under which these Indian converts were clustered about the missions—protected, industrious, well fed and well clothed, with their herds, flocks, gardens, and orchards spreading out under the shadow of the focal object, the mission church. So correctly placed were these mission settlements from the geographic point of view, that the succeeding years witnessed the growth around them, or in close proximity to them, of a number of the most important cities of the State, including Los Angeles and San Francisco and also Monterey—the seat of the beloved mission of San Carlos de Carmel and the capital, civil and religious, of California for nearly eighty years. And what is equally marvelous SERRA, in determining upon mission sites, invariably and yet seemingly without the advantage of any previous knowledge, selected sites which later experience demonstrated to be the most fertile of each locality.

But the passing years and physical infirmity took their toll—and SERRA at the age of more than three score years and ten departed this life in 1784, within the precincts of the mission at Carmel. No vaulted, pretentious repository for his remains! Rather, a quiet space beneath the old arches of San Carlos de Carmel, fashioned by rude native hands. So afflicted at his death were his protégés, the Indians, that, it is said, they fought for shreds of his poor friar's robe and for fragments of his whitened hair.

The retreating decades, however, were no more mindful of him than they have been of others among the great. In time even the sanctuary of his grave was violated by gathering débris. But, fortunately, a later generation—coming after the time of the vandals, and their efforts to efface the work of the missions—bethought itself of this great and singular man, and of his accomplishments, and to-day the cult of SERRA is full ripe again in the length and breadth of California.

A worthy chronicler of California's romantic days, John Steven McGroarty, pens this appreciation of the civilizing friar:

> During the sixteen years of JUNIPERO'S labors in California, nine missions had been established, either directly by himself or under his direction. In those missions were five thousand eight hundred Indian neophytes whom he had converted, with the assistance of his companions,

from heathenism to Christianity. This number of people whom he had found living worse than the lives of dogs he left in a new world of light and health and joy. He had taught the hand of the savage to do a Christian white man's work, to sing Christian music and speak prayers. Within the valleys and the sun-swept hills where he had found only waste and desolation he left unnumbered flocks and herds. It is perhaps quite safe to say that there is not in all the history of civilization one other single man whose individual labors for God and humanity bore such a bountiful harvest. The name of JUNIPERO SERRA is to-day the best-loved name in California, without distinction of class or creed. His memory is honored and revered by all the people.

It is estimated that at one time more than thirty thousand Indian converts were lodged in the mission buildings, receiving religious instructions, assisting at divine worship, and cheerfully performing their easy tasks.

Fellow citizens, I take it to be axiomatic that our Nation pays tribute where tribute is due. I take it to be axiomatic that achievement is the only true justification for commemorative tribute. I take it to be equally axiomatic that no nation so much as our Nation pays commemorative tribute to achievement, particularly achievement amid discouragement and difficulty and poverty. I take it that no immortal in this hall should be deemed more "worthy of this national commemoration" than JUNIPERO SERRA.

In the midst of hurrying days and shifting human scenes, so in contrast with the simpler past, he stands—this Padre JUNIPERO SERRA—as in a mellow sanctuary light of the eternal, blended with the mundane. His inextinguishable mark is upon the face of California. He is California's apostle to the Indians. He is our country's first civilizer of our western coast. He justly stands, for the edification of future generations, among the immortals of our Nation.

It was of such a man as this, that Solomon in all his wisdom, sang—

> His memory shall not recede, and his name shall be looked for from generation to generation.

The United States Marine Band played another selection.

The PRESIDING OFFICER. We are privileged in having Hon. Samuel M. Shortridge, Senator from California, depict the life and history of one of America's foremost citizens, THOMAS STARR KING. Senator M. Shortridge.

ADDRESS BY SENATOR SHORTRIDGE

Grateful for the rare privilege, California presents these, her two beloved and cherished sons, to the Nation, here to stand alongside of others who have rendered great service to our country. Each in his day served God and man. Though dead, they speak. Their works, their lives, will ever be a blessing and an inspiration. Missionary and minister, they held aloft the celestial banner of God and the heavenly flag of the Republic.

Of the one you have just heard; of the other I would briefly speak.

Thomas Starr King was born in New York City December 17, 1824, the eldest child of a scholarly father and a gifted mother. The father, T. Farrington King, became pastor of a Universalist Society at Portsmouth, N. H., where the son passed six years of early boyhood; later, in 1835, the family moved to and lived in Charlestown, Mass. At the early age of eighteen years he became principal of a grammar school in Medford, Mass. To assist the family, in 1843 he obtained a position as bookkeeper in the Charlestown Navy Yard.

At the age of twenty years he began to preach, delivering his first sermon in Woburn, Mass. Later he occupied pulpits in Boston. In 1846 he was pastor of a Charlestown parish, and in 1848 he was installed as pastor of the Hollis Street Society, a Unitarian denomination, where he served for eleven years.

During this period of his life, Thomas Starr King achieved a great reputation for goodness and for greatness. To him duty was indeed the voice of God, and to that voice he ever harkened. The learned acknowledged him as an equal, and the lowly, the poor, the outcast, sought and received his aid and comfort.

In 1859 he received an earnest call from the far West, and, with the missionary spirit, answered that call and journeyed by way of the Isthmus of Panama to California, entering its Golden Gate on April 28, 1860. Immediately entering upon his sacred calling as minister of the Unitarian Church in San Francisco, he continued to make that city his home until, alas, too soon, he closed his eyes in eternal sleep.

I would have you know him as we knew him. He was frail in body, but transcendently great in mind. Gentle, affectionate, unassuming, happy when serving, and endowed with a marvelous gift of speech, he quickly won the love and admiration of our people. He was indeed golden-tongued. In addition to his ministerial duties he delivered many splendid addresses on scientific, literary, and historical subjects, journeying through California and our sister States of Oregon and Washington and on into British Columbia.

It can be said in very truth that THOMAS STARR KING fell in love with California and that California fell in love with him. No pen, no tongue, has more vividly or more eloquently described and portrayed the physical glories of that State than did the pen and tongue of this reverend man.

But you may ask me why we loved him; why we exalt him; why we place him in bronze here in the Capitol of the Republic. Soon after his coming to California the battle of brothers, the Civil War, broke out. THOMAS STARR KING hated no man, no State, but oh how he reverenced the Constitution and loved the Republic. He flung himself in a spirit of loyalty to the defense of the flag of Washington and Jefferson and Jackson and Lincoln. By day and by night, across valleys and through mountain passes, in sunshine and storm, he traveled and appealed in behalf of the Union. Nobler or more eloquent appeals were never made in behalf of the Republic. Wearied, he never faltered; and though warned by his friends, he never rested during those dark and doubtful days.

And then, like Moses in sight of the promised land—in sight of the Republic's triumphant flag—in sight of a Union saved—in sight of a reunited Republic—in sight of peace—he died. He died on March 4, 1864. Thus from the cradle to the grave he traveled but forty years. He passed into the higher life with a smile on his lips, repeating in a clear, well modulated voice, the Twenty-third Psalm—"The Lord is my shepherd, I shall not want. Yea, though I walk through the valley and the shadow of death I will fear no evil for Thou art with me, Thy rod and Thy staff they comfort me." California wept; the Nation wept.

Though dead, he speaks to us and he enjoins upon us to be faithful to the Republic in the service of which he died. For even as the soldier falls on the battle field, so THOMAS STARR KING laid down his life for the Union.

God grant that we of California and of the Nation may be worthy inheritors of his labors. God grant that this Republic may be true to the principles for which he stood.

"America" was rendered by the United States Marine Band.

The Presiding Officer. It is a pleasure to present Mrs. William Elmer Evans, wife of Congressman Evans, of California, who will pay a brief tribute to these illustrious men of California and present wreaths in the name of the California Federation of Women's Clubs. Mrs. William Elmer Evans.

REMARKS BY MRS. EVANS

The purple lupines and the yellow poppies along the gentle slopes of El Camino Real softened many a weary mile for the bare feet of this beloved Spanish padre as he walked back and forth between the crescent bay of San Diego in the south and the Golden Gate of San Francisco in the north teaching the people of his missions.

So, to-day, on behalf of the California Federation of Women's Clubs, it is my great privilege to lay at these feet of bronze this wreath of California wild flowers.

THOMAS STARR KING did perhaps the greatest service of all for posterity by helping to preserve California to the Union. Not only California but every State from the Atlantic to the Pacific should delight to honor this man as we, the California Federation of Women's Clubs, place at his bronze feet this wreath of forty-eight red and white roses, tied with the blue, symbolic of the American flag which California, though of Spanish traditions, is proud to claim and to honor.

The PRESIDING OFFICER. The Native Sons and Native Daughters of the Golden West have been particularly interested and helpful in securing the legislation to make this day possible, and it is, therefore, fitting on this occasion that these organizations participate in a humble way in expressing their appreciation of JUNIPERO SERRA and THOMAS STARR KING. I have asked Hon. Arthur M. Free to represent the Native Sons and Native Daughters of the Golden West.

ADDRESS BY REPRESENTATIVE FREE

I have been requested to appear here to-day on behalf of the Native Sons and Native Daughters of the Golden West. To those who are not informed, may I state that these two great organizations are composed of those men and women who have had the privilege of being born within the confines of the State of California, and have associated themselves in a fraternal bond of friendship with the specific purposes of earnestly and carefully studying the history of California, perpetuating this history and the traditions of the State, and of studying and perpetuating the memory of her pioneers.

As a part of their work these organizations have undertaken to keep in a reasonable state of preservation, the missions founded under the direction of one of the characters whom we are here to honor to-day, and which represent the gathering places for the earliest civilization of California and the dissemination of the Christian religion.

California has an interesting and colorful background. Originally it was under the jurisdiction of Spain, later it came under Mexican domination, and then those pioneers who had gathered in this far-away land, coming either by boat, or ox team, or by crossing the Isthmus of Panama, decided to establish an independent republic, and after this republic had been fully organized, then through its properly constituted authorities, it appealed to the Government of the United States of America that it might be made a part and parcel of the United States.

Transportation in those days was slow, mail moved slowly and irregularly, and much time elapsed between the sending of this petition to the National Capitol at Washington, D. C., and the receipt of the response thereto, but finally on October 18, 1850, the old side-wheeler, the *Oregon,* came into San Francisco Harbor with the news that California, which had never experienced territorial childhood, had been accepted into the sisterhood of States.

Junipero Serra peculiarly concerned several of these periods in California history. He was born at Petra, on the island of Majorca (a province of Spain). As a young man he migrated to Mexico and thence to California. He went on foot from San Diego to San Francisco, established missions which were built out of adobe by the hands of the Indians who populated the various sections, and these missions for many years served as places for the dissemination of information, served as a background for the establishment of a new civilization in these parts and also were the gathering places where Christianity as he saw it was proclaimed.

Thomas Starr King likewise played a very important part in California history. Born in New York City, he migrated to California just at the time of the outbreak of the Civil War. It was not certain where California would cast her lot in this struggle, but King, through his eloquence, pleaded with the peoples of that State to remain loyal to the Union, and it was to him, perhaps, more than any other individual that the credit is due for California remaining in the sisterhood of States.

If you were to go with me to our State capitol, located in the great Sacramento Valley in the central portion of California, I could point out to you a portrait of this great man and beneath it are these words, "The man whose matchless oratory saved California to the Union." Or, if you would go with me into Golden Gate Park located in the city of San Francisco where the kindly waters of the Pacific bathe the western shores of these United States, there in the midst of beautiful flowers and resplendent verdure you would see another likeness of this man, a statue under which is written, "In him eloquence, strength, and virtue were devoted with fearless courage to truth, country, and his fellow man." And so to-day we have unveiled another statue to him in this hall where only a few can be so greatly honored.

I wish sometime you could come with me out to the State of California, particularly to the district which I have the pleasure to represent, and I would take you to the old town of Monterey which I have the honor not only to represent in the Congress of the United States, but to appear to-day as her representative at these ceremonies, and I would go with you to a promontory overlooking the beautiful Monterey Bay and there I would show you a monument erected in memory of JUNIPERO SERRA holding forth a cross symbolic of the Christianity in which he believed and taught to the natives of my beloved State, his eyes turned toward heaven as though pleading to the great God of us all for the welfare of the State where he spent so many years of his life, and there with an expression of welcome looking out on the great Pacific welcoming others to that land of sunshine and plenty as he had done in life, ah, and even now welcoming all who might care to come to carry on the work which he so successfully undertook and to develop this great State.

Then I would take you but a few miles away into one of the beautiful valleys of which California is renowned, the Carmel Valley, and there I would point out to you an old mission established in 1771, built by the loving hands of faithful followers of JUNIPERO SERRA. I could show you some of the walls which have begun to crumble, but still intact the little church with its melodious bells which called the Indians to service and to study, and its old pews crudely but substantially made, with its altar and the stones upon which the faithful followers have trod these many years, somewhat worn; and then I would lead you into a little sanctuary, modest, unostentatious, simple, a mere slab of stone placed upon mother earth, and here I would point out to you the last earthly resting place of JUNIPERO SERRA.

As the representative of the Native Sons and Native Daughters of the Golden West it affords me unusual pleasure to be present here to-day and to do honor to these two characters who played such an important part in the early history of our beloved State.

Miss Stoermer, past grand president of the Native Daughters of the Golden West, paid a brief tribute to these men and presented beautiful flowers in the name of that organization.

139696—32——5

STATUES OF SERRA AND KING

The PRESIDING OFFICER. It is indeed a pleasure and a delightful surprise to have Father Seraphin Muller, O. F. M., of the mission at Santa Barbara, Calif., here to-day. He has been sent as a special representative of the Franciscan Order of California and will pay a tribute to the beloved founder of the California missions. Father Seraphin Muller.

ADDRESS BY FATHER MULLER

Coming from Old Mission Santa Barbara and representing the Franciscan Friars of California, who are the successors of the Spanish padres of old, I wish to say that we consider it a great privilege that the first of our brethren to set foot upon Californian soil should be honored by having his statue placed in our National Capitol in National Statuary Hall.

It is not without coincidence that in this unveiling ceremony the statue of Friar JUNIPERO SERRA should face that of George Washington. At first sight there may seem to be no common bond of union between the Father of our Country and the Apostle of California, but they were contemporaries and if we look into the history of their day in the light of later events we see that they worked for a common cause.

It was in the year 1769 that JUNIPERO SERRA first came to California and founded Mission San Diego, the first of the twenty-one jewels that dot El Camino Real from San Diego to Sonoma, and at that time agitation for freedom was growing strong in the Colonies. In the year 1776, the year of the Declaration of Independence, JUNIPERO SERRA founded the mission of San Francisco beside the Golden Gate. By the time of his death in 1784 a new nation had been born.

So it happened that while General Washington and his patriots fought for the existence of our country, JUNIPERO SERRA and his band of friars brought Christianity and civilization to California in preparation for its subsequent admission into the Unon. At that time between the Atlantic and the Pacific lay the French colonies and a vast wilderness. I doubt if General Washington in his wildest imagination ever looked to the Golden West, and I doubt if JUNIPERO SERRA's thoughts ever went beyond the Sierra Nevada Mountains. Yet each oblivious of the other, under the guidance of Providence was working for a common cause—these greater United States of our day that stretch from the Atlantic to the Pacific.

The unveiling of the statue of JUNIPERO SERRA is the realization of the words spoken by the Hon. Hiram W. Johnson when on the 24th of November, 1913, the bicentennial of the birth of JUNIPERO SERRA, as Governor of the State of California he proclaimed a legal holiday saying: "To the memory of JUNIPERO SERRA California owes an everlasting tribute. He brought civilization to our land, and in deed and character he deserves a foremost place in the history of our State."

The PRESIDING OFFICER. Floral tributes will be presented to Father JUNIPERO SERRA by Hon. Richard J. Welch, Representative in Congress from the Fifth District of California at the request of the mayor of San Francisco and the Knights of Columbus. Hon. Richard J. Welch.

REMARKS BY REPRESENTATIVE WELCH

I have been honored by the requests of Hon. Angelo J. Rossi, mayor of the city of San Francisco, acting for the people of San Francisco, and of Harry W. McGowan, state deputy, representing the California jurisdiction of the Knights of Columbus, to pay the respects of the city of San Francisco and of the Knights of Columbus to this distinguished assemblage and to present these beautiful floral offerings as their tributes to Father JUNIPERO SERRA at the unveiling of the statue of the beloved founder of California's missions in Statuary Hall in the United States Capitol.

JUNIPERO SERRA founded Mission Dolores in San Francisco (the city of St. Francis) in the year 1776. His name is revered by every true Californian, regardless of race or creed, and his memory will last as long as the sun sets on California's shores.

The PRESIDING OFFICER. Hon. Florence Prag Kahn will present a tribute to THOMAS STARR KING.

Mrs. KAHN. I place this wreath with the love, appreciation, and reverence of San Francisco, the city in which he labored and lived.

The PRESIDING OFFICER. A rare privilege is mine to-day, for I have the honor of presenting to you the men who have labored earnestly and effectively to execute in bronze the figures of the men California has chosen to honor.

Mr. Ettore Cadorin, of Santa Barbara, the sculptor of JUNIPERO SERRA.

Mr. Haig Patigian, of San Francisco, the sculptor of THOMAS STARR KING.

The United States Marine Band played "I Love You, California."

Rev. Ulysses Grant Pierce, pastor of All Souls Unitarian Church, of Washington, D. C., pronounced the benediction.

"Stars and Stripes Forever" was played by the Marine Band.

ACCEPTANCE
of the STATUES

By the Senate, February 23, 1931
By the House, February 27, 1931

PROCEEDINGS IN THE SENATE

MONDAY, *February 23, 1931.*

Mr. SHORTRIDGE submitted a concurrent resolution (S. Con. Res. 40), which was considered by unanimous consent and agreed to, as follows:

Resolved by the Senate (the House of Representatives concurring), That the statues of JUNIPERO SERRA and THOMAS STARR KING, presented by the State of California, to be placed in Statuary Hall, are accepted in the name of the United States, and that the thanks of Congress be tendered said State for the contribution of the statues of these eminent men, illustrious for their distinguished services as pioneer patriots of said State.

Resolved further, That a copy of these resolutions, suitably engrossed and duly authenticated, be transmitted to the Governor of California.

SATURDAY, *February 28, 1931.*

A message from the House of Representatives, by Mr. Chaffee, one of its clerks, announced that the House had agreed to the concurrent resolution (S. Con. Res. 40) accepting the statues of JUNIPERO SERRA and THOMAS STARR KING, to be placed in Statuary Hall.

PROCEEDINGS IN THE HOUSE

TUESDAY, *February 24, 1931.*

A message from the Senate, by Mr. Craven, its principal clerk, announced that the Senate had passed a concurrent resolution (S. Con. Res. 40) accepting the statues of JUNIPERO SERRA and THOMAS STARR KING, to be placed in Statuary Hall, in which the concurrence of the House is requested.

FRIDAY, *February 27, 1931.*

Mr. LUCE. Mr. Speaker, I ask unanimous consent for the present consideration of a concurrent resolution, Senate Concurrent Resolution 40.

The SPEAKER. The gentleman from Massachusetts asks unanimous consent for the present consideration of a Senate concurrent resolution, which the Clerk will report.

The Clerk read the Senate concurrent resolution, as follows:

Resolved by the Senate (the House of Representatives concurring), That the statues of JUNIPERO SERRA and THOMAS STARR KING, presented by the State of California to be placed in Statuary Hall, are accepted in the name of the United States, and that the thanks of Congress be tendered said State for the contribution of the statues of these eminent men, illustrious for their distinguished services as pioneer patriots of said State.

Resolved further, That a copy of these resolutions, suitably engrossed and duly authenticated, be transmitted to the Governor of California.

The concurrent resolution was agreed to.

www.ingramcontent.com/pod-product-compliance
Lightning Source LLC
LaVergne TN
LVHW020655100826
845148LV00012B/2509

* 9 7 8 0 9 4 4 2 8 5 7 8 7 *